Anonymous

A Letter to the Right Honourable Lord North

Anonymous

A Letter to the Right Honourable Lord North

ISBN/EAN: 9783337059248

Printed in Europe, USA, Canada, Australia, Japan

Cover: Foto ©ninafisch / pixelio.de

More available books at **www.hansebooks.com**

A

LETTER

To the RIGHT HONOURABLE

LORD NORTH.

My Lord,

I Gave all the attention due to the importance of the subject, and to your Lordship's great abilities, when on the 5th of April you opened to the House of Commons a proposition, tending to permit the territorial acquisitions and revenues, lately obtained in India, to remain, under proper restrictions and regulations, in the

B   possession

poſſeſſion of the Company, during a term not exceeding ſix years; the public to forego all participation in the produce thereof, until the Company ſhall have repaid ſuch ſums of money as ſhall be advanced by the public for the relief of the Company, and the bond-debt of the Company be reduced to 1,500,000 l. from thenceforth, during the remainder of the ſaid term, three fourth parts of the ſurplus nett profits of the Company at home, above the ſum of 8 l. *per cent. per annum,* upon their capital ſtock, to be paid into the Exchequer, for the uſe of the public; and the remaining fourth part to be applied, either in further reducing the Company's bond-debt, or for compoſing a fund to be ſet apart for the uſe of the Company in the caſe of extraordinary emergencies.

Such is the ſubſtance, and nearly ſuch, were the words, of your Lordſhip's motion. The Company can be ſupported by no means ſhort of thoſe propoſed by you for their preſent relief. The terms of
participation

participation are certainly equal to what they can, in any degree of moderation, expect. Nay, I think, they exceed every reasonable expectation which the Company could form, and that the public have a just claim upon the whole of that fourth remaining part, which, in the question and the resolution upon it, is to be applied either in further reducing the Company's bond-debt, or to the use of the Company in extraordinary emergencies.

Although, upon a medium of many years back, the Company have divided 8l. *per cent.* and fallacious calculations have been produced to justify such excessive dividends; yet it is certain that these profits, fairly stated, did not entitle them to divide above six. An addition of 2l. *per cent.* principally arising out of the territorial revenue, now acknowledged to belong to the public, will surely be sufficient for the Company.

Were the surplus fourth to be appropriated to an increase of the Company's

capital

capital in trade, as your Lordſhip, in your
ſpeech, wiſhed it might, and you called
upon the Houſe for the opinion of other
members upon that ſubject; ſuch increaſe,
while it augmented the revenue of the
public, would accumulate profits, which,
although they could not be applied to the
immediate benefit of the Company in an
increaſe of dividend, muſt become their
property, whenever their agreement with
the public ſhould ceaſe. In the poſſible
ſuppoſition that the trade might not admit
of an increaſed capital, proviſion ſhould
ſurely be made for lending that fourth
part to the public, at a very moderate rate
of intereſt, if any at all ſhould be thought
reaſonable. But as your Lordſhip's invi-
tation to the members, to declare their
opinion upon the moſt proper purpoſes to
which that ſurplus might be applied, was
not accepted, the queſtion paſſed in the
original words of the motion ; and I much
fear, that *extraordinary emergencies* can
never be interpreted to mean that increaſe

of

of capital, from which alone the public can derive any advantage. Such emergencies may much more probably hereafter arife from, and be conftrued to mean, the Company's bond-debts in the Indies, which, by accounts received from India fince your Lordfhip's fpeech on the 5th of April, amount to 1,416,000 l. Thefe have not been taken into your Lordfhip's contemplation, nor into any of the calculations formed upon the ftate of the Company. No provifion has been made for their difcharge; nay, their amount, until now, was not precifely known. No reftrictions appear to be thought on, to prevent their increafe; nor can it be faid with certainty, that emergencies may not arife in India to render an increafe of debt neceffary. Yet the creditors of the Company there have, and will have, as good a claim as thofe in Europe, who have lent fums to the Company, which they had no right to borrow. Equity and compaffion will be equally ftrong in both cafes, and law but equally weak.

I have

I have dwelt thus long upon the impropriety of applying the surplus profits to the use of the Company, not so much from a belief that they will become an object much worthy of attention during the remainder of the Company's term, as from an apprehenſion that ſuch a precedent may be prejudicial to the public in any future bargain with the preſent or any other Company.

I have no doubt of your Lordſhip's induſtry in enquiring into the nature of the evils to be remedied, and in deviſing the beſt means to eradicate them, and prevent their return.

But, forgive me for ſaying it, I as little doubt the impoſſibility, by any regulations which can be formed, of curing evils ſo interewoven with the original conſtitution of the Company, as, in the words of the Poet, to " grow with their growth, " and ſtrengthen with their ſtrength." In ſuch caſes, if you would eradicate the evils, you muſt deſtroy the patient. Their exiſtence is coeval and inſeparable.

The

The evils to be cured are, gambling in the alley, and frauds and malverfations at home and abroad.

The caufes are felf-evident: an open and indifcriminate admiffion of all defcriptions of men, and a right in fuch men, under certain real or fictitious qualifications, to choofe their Directors, and after fuch choice to controll their councils and actions, during the fhort continuance to which their exiftence is limited. Thefe caufes were admitted into the original formation of the Company, and became a part of its effence: remove thefe, and you annihilate the Company. But while this Company remains, the evils arifing from thofe caufes muft exift. They grew as the Company flourifhed; but, feeding upon its vitals in proportion as the nourifhment increafed, they confumed that fupply, by which both were fupported: They now decline together; and will rife together, if the Company fhould ever revive. Palliatives may be ufed, temporary expedients

dients may be tried : ſuch have been uſed and tried; and every further endeavour will only ſerve to prove the inefficacy and futility of ſuch attempts, while the cauſe remains rooted and untouched.

As the poſſeſſions of the Company were extended in India, the Direction increaſed in importance, and became after their acquiſition of the territorial revenues one of the great objects of avarice, ambition, and party ; artifice, fraud, and corruption, means uſual and natural to them, were employed to operate upon the body of electors, then compoſed of men moſt fuſceptible of their impreſſions: the ſober, honeſt, and diſcreet Proprietors of the late liſts retired from the Company, ſatisfied with a large and unexpected increaſe of fortune; and were ſucceeded by adventurers and gameſters, a fluctuating ſet, who bought in or ſold out as their ever-varying ſpeculations directed them.

The body of Directors, whoſe annual election depended upon ſuch conſtituents, were

were equally fubject to viciffitude and change: in the numberlefs fhiftings of Proprietors new men were to be gratified; and in every change of Directors the friends of thofe difplaced were to be won over by new gratifications. In either event the intereft of the publick was facrificed, and the plunder of the Indies made the reward and wages of corrupt fervices, while the uncertainty of the tenure fpread quicker and wider the fcenes of cruelty and devaftation.

It may not be improper here to infert Lord Clive's defcription of the General Courts and the Court of Directors, with which he clofed his fpeech in the Houfe of Commons on the 30th March 1772.

" With regard to the General Courts I believe I need not dwell long on the confequence of them. Their violent pro-ceedings have been fubverfive of the authority of the Court of Directors. The agents abroad have known this: They have therefore never fcrupled to fet the

C   orders

orders of Directors at defiance, when it was their interest to disobey them; and they have escaped punishment, by means of the over-awing interest of individuals at General Courts. Thus have General Courts co-operated with the Court of Directors in the mischiefs that have arisen in Bengal; whilst annual contested elections have in a manner deprived the Directors of the power of establishing any authority over their servants. The first half of the year is employed in freeing themselves from the obligations contracted by their last election; and the second half is wasted in incurring new obligations, and securing their election for the next year, by daily sacrifices of some interest of the Company. The Direction, notwithstanding all these manœuvres, has been so fluctuating and unsettled, that new and contradictory orders have been frequently sent out; and the servants, who to say the truth have generally understood the interest of the Company much

much better than the Directors, have in many instances followed their own opinion, in opposition to theirs."

Yet great as the evils have been arising from an annual choice of Directors, a prolongation of their term would be a hazardous expedient, until a better mode of choosing shall ensure a better choice.

The surprising turn of events, by which the Company was snatched from the brink of destruction and raised to the throne of Aurungzebe in the most flourishing part of his dominions, is too well known to require a repetition here, even were it necessary to my present purpose. The causes which have since produced another reverse, equally astonishing, are various and numberless. Many of them are still hidden in the obscurity natural and necessary to guilt; but the fatal effects are notorious: The Company is bankrupt, and India is ruined. Nations rise to prosperity and affluence by slow degrees; but their fall may be sudden and precipitate. The late

C 2   flourish-

flourishing state of India was the work
of ages: the desolation now spread over
it, is, as we have seen, the operation of
a very few years; while Britain, far from
being enriched, is impoverished by its
spoils.

The scenes of villainy and horror, de-
scribed in Fielding's Life of Jonathan
Wild the Great, have been realized and
heightened there; so far will avarice and
rapacity surpass all the creative powers of
invention, in the pursuit of their objects.
The miscreant actors who started up into Nabobs in India, are since become Lords
of no inconsiderable possessions in Great
Britain; and some are become legislators
here, who, by all laws human and divine,
would for far less crimes committed in
any civilized country, be punished there
with imprisonment, confiscation, and
death.

But India became lawless from the
moment she passed under our government;
the sceptre, wrested from the gentle grasp

of

of Afiatic defpotifm, was thrown afide, and rods of iron put into the hands of Britifh barbarians : No rule for direction, no fanction for punifhment, no intereft in the rulers for the protection and perfervation of the governed, prevailed there. The harveft was abundant, but the feafon fhort and precarious : not a moment was loft in gathering, not an art was omitted that could expedite the hoarding. Pride and emulation ftimulated avarice ; and the fole conteft was, who fhould return to that home, which they almoft all quitted beggars, with the greateft heap of crimes and of plunder.

The firft labourers tired and fatiated left the gleanings to others, who are fince fucceffively returned with fmaller, but not inconfiderable; bundles ; and the only men left deftitute are the unhappy natives, to whom the whole of right belonged.

Wealth operates on a nation as food on the animal body : to give ftrength and health, it muft gradually diffufe itfelf, properly

perly prepared and digefted, over all the
parts through an infinite variety of channels. Too great a quantity thrown in at
once over-charges the fyftem, ftops the
paffages, and interrupts circulation; producing difeafe, langour, and death.

Wealth acquired by manufacture and
commerce, the earnings of all ranks of
men from the labourer up to the mer-
chant-exporter, will enrich all with pro-
portional fhares of profit and reward;
while a fudden influx, poured in by rapine
and fraud, choaks the channels of induftry, deluging and impoverifhing the
face of that country which they were
wont to fertilize. Such was the fate of
Rome when Carthage was plundered; and
fuch have been the confequences derived
to Great Britain, from Eaft-India devaftation.

Although the heavy diftreffes under
which we continue to labour, have had
their commencement with the frauds and
mifconduct of the Company, and the enormities

mities committed by their fervants; although the loffes and ruin of thoufands in thefe kingdoms proceed evidently and immediately from that polluted fource; yet there have been other concurrent caufes, and it would not be fair to lay the whole of our calamitous fituation to the charge of one of thofe caufes only, although it may have mixed with and aggravated our misfortunes in every other inftance.

The fame inclement winds blowing from the eaft would have blafted our harvefts, and ftunted our cattle, although they had not wafted thofe fwarms of locufts to us. But increafed confumption produces greater fcarcity; and gold lavifhed in feducing the laborious to idlenefs, and fpreading the contagion of vicious example, increafes price, while it difcourages induftry.

If the company could be faved for the benefit of the public, they cannot be in better hands than your Lordfhip's. *Si Pergama dextra defendi poffent, etiam hac de-*

3   *fenfa*

fenfa fuiffent. And this will be the only comfort of much toil and difappointed labour, which will remain with your Lordfhip, in your attempts to refcue from deferved ruin a race of ignorant and wicked barbarians, offenfive to heaven and earth.

I do not mean to include under this defcription of the aggregate body every individual of which it is compofed, among whom there are, no doubt, many, who, free from the crimes of their affociates, are not difgraced by being members of fuch a community. Some there certainly are, who, while they have acquired wealth by honeft means, have with a Gregory and a Haftings gained no lefs honour by an avowed difapprobation of thofe who have enriched themfelves by fraud and rapine.

The formation of the Eaft India Company, ill adapted even to the narrow object of their firft inftitution, became abfolutely incompatible with the elevated fituation to which they have been fince raifed.

If it was ill-judged to truft the choice of Directors, who had only a few fmall factories

ries to govern in India, and a trade not very confiderable to direct, to a company compofed of all forts of men, the impropriety of fuch a mode of election became greater as the truft grew more important, the electors lefs fit to be confided in, and the temptations to a wrong choice incomparably ftronger. The trade to the Eaft Indies, even as it ftood in the reign of Elizabeth, when we had no poffeffions there, when our capital did not exceed 26,000 l. nor our fhipping one thoufand four hundred and thirty tons, fhould not have been trufted to Directors chofen by fuch men as ftand qualified to vote upon the prefent lift of Proprietors. But that fuch men fhould choofe not only the Directors of the moft extenfive and important trade known to the mercantile world, but that the fame vote fhould raife them to arbitrary dominion over an empire, containing from fifteen to feventeen millions of inhabitants, and that every year the fame mode of election fhould be repeated, is an

D   abfurdity

abfurdity not to be paralleled in any time, or in any country.

It is true, that all are admitted to purchafe ftock in the Dutch Eaft-India Company; and although the whole of their capital be but about 600,000 l. upon which the dividend is, at a medium, about 15 *per cent.* nearly five of which is paid in the firft place to the States; and although none of thofe furprifing revolutions have happened in their Eaft-India poffeffions, which have opened that wide field of fpeculation that has drawn adventurers from all parts of Europe into our company; yet gamblers in Dutch Eaft-India ftock are not unknown in the United Provinces. The numbers indeed are few, and the evils confined within a narrow compafs. But were the holders of Dutch ftock, under certain money'd qualifications, entrufted with an annual choice of their Directors, who, like ours, are fovereigns in India, and with a conftant control over them; inconfiderable as the fums are, to which their ftock and dividend

dend amount, the offices to be difpofed of in Batavia, and the other extenfive Dutch fettlements in India, under the influence of fuch conftituents over the creatures of their choice, would deluge the Dutch pofleffions with the fame enormities that have deftroyed Bengal, and would fpread over the United Provinces the fame misfortunes which have lately overtaken fome of their inhabitants, lefs cautious adventurers in our Eaft-India ftock than their wary countrymen have been, and are wont to be.

Whoever perufes the lift of our Proprietors will fee by the quantity of ftock poffeffed by each, calculated as qualifications to choofe and for being chofen Directors, that elections are the object to which the general attention was entirely directed. Their hopes and expectations arofe from an unjuft and partial adminiftration, favourable to them and their friends; not from a wife and honeft conduct, equally beneficial to all : they trufted to peculation, and not to fair profit ;

D 2   while

while Nabobs, placing the immenfe bulk of their fortune in other fecurities, beyond the reach of that tottering edifice whofe foundations they had fapped, left juft enough behind to entitle them to fhare in the property and difpofal of the materials of the ruin.

The Proprietors of ftock, in Holland, have not the choice of their Directors, nor have any but the Directors a decifive voice in the management of affairs. Upon the death of a Director, for the Directors are continued for life, thofe of the Chamber where the vacancy happens, and who mean to be prefent at the election, fummon an equal number of Proprietors, poffeffed of about 550l. ftock, to attend, and to concur with them in the nomination of three perfons of the Company, out of whom a fucceffor to the deceafed is chofen by the Sovereign, who has alfo a voice, by his reprefentative, in each of the fix Chambers. Seven Proprietors are admitted into the affembly of 17 Directors,

tors, deputed by all the Chambers, to
meet twice a year; thofe Proprietors may
make any propofitions they think proper,
and deliver their opinions upon any fubject
propofed; but they have no vote in the
decifion of any controverted queftions.
Here end the functions of the meer Dutch
ftock-holder, with refpect to the general
concerns of the Company; and, thus re-
ftrained from any influence over the Directors, and from any management of the
Company's affairs, it is of little importance, with refpect to thefe objects, who
they are who compofe the body of Proprietors in Holland. But it is far other-
wife in our Company; and I will venture
to affert, that, while elections remain in
the body of Proprietors, whatever the money'd qualifications may be made, no regulations or reftrictions that can be devifed
will prove fufficient.

Thofe reftrictions and regulations muft
either originate in Parliament, or in the
Company. But, wherever they take their

rife,

rife, they fhould be confirmed, and their
duration fecured, by Parliamentary authority; and this fhould be done in the very
firft inftance, as proper regulations and reftrictions are, in the queftion of the 5th of
April, made the condition under which
the poffeffion of the territorial revenues is
to remain with the Company during a
term not exceeding fix years.

If the condition be not accomplifhed,
and the regulations and reftrictions expref-
fly and compleatly fettled at the time that
the grant to the Company is made, it muft
remain refumable upon non-performance;
and fhould the whole or any confiderable
part be fuffered to reft upon the precarious ground of the Company's by-laws,
uncertainty and infecurity will be the natural confequences, in both cafes; and
thefe, in their turn, will produce the fame
fpirit of gambling and adventure which
has already proved fo very fatal.

Yet, my Lord, it will be impoffible in
this feffion of parliament to perfect that

great

great work of legiflation. The Company never can do it: they are equally unfit to enact or to execute. Thofe among them, who know moft, are the leaft fit to be advifed with: they are the authors of thofe very mifchiefs you would redrefs. Yet, in the printed fpeech of their noble apologift, page 42 to 46, " The Company's fervants have not been the authors of thofe acts of violence and oppreffion of which it is the fafhion to accufe them. Such crimes were committed by the natives of the country acting as their agents, and for the moft part without their knowledge," until " they were dragged into the kennel by thofe agents and Banyans:" then indeed they began to know fomething of the matter, for, " then the acts of violence begin." The Banyan, charming as a fair lady to the Company's fervants, lays his bags of filver before him to-day, gold to-morrow, jewels the next day; and if thefe fail, he then tempts him in the way of his profeffion, which is trade. The Company's fervant has no refource, for he cannot fly. In fhort, flefh and blood cannot bear it. Thus are poor Englifh youths of fixteen fent out by the Company to be writers, not worth a groat, corrupted in their principles at their very firft fetting out, left at the mercy of Banyans and in a ftate of dependence under them, who commit fuch acts of violence and oppreffion as their intereft prompts them to, under the pretended fanction and authority of the Company's fervant." Good God! what muft thofe Directors be, who fend out fuch boys in ftations which command fuch influence! And what muft thofe intrufted with power in India be, who permit its exercife! But wonder will ceafe, when we confider, that Directors muft bind their conftitu-ents to them by obligations, ftronger in proportion to the unfitnefs of the perfon recommended and preferred; and that the fervants of the Company in high ftations rofe by the fame fteps, and learned in the

fame

fame fchools those admirable maxims of
government, which they ever after prac-
tifed. Hence, exclaims our author, " ari-
fes the clamour againft the Englifh Gentlemen in India." Poor Gentlemen!
while our hearts bleed for the oppreffion
and dependance under which they groaned
in India, dragged through kennels, heavi-
ly loaded with filver, gold, jewels, and
precious merchandife by cruel Banyans;
we are at length relieved in page 46, by
the pleafing picture of thofe *Englifh Gentlemen*, releafed from their captivity, " in
a retired fituation when returned to Eng-
land, where they are no longer Nabobs
and Sovereigns of the Eaft; nothing tyrannical in their difpofitions towards their
inferiors:" poffibly the tables kept for
their upper fervants, may have been open
to the late proprietors of the houfes which
they inhabit. " Good and humane mafters to their fervants;" fome of whom
they formerly ferved in the loweft ftations. " Charitable, benevolent, gener-

E   ous

ous and hospitable," to every poor bo-
rough that would shake off the yoke of
natural interest. " Not one character suf-
ficiently flagitious for Mr. Foote to exhi-
bit on the Theatre in the Hay-market."
Here his Lordship mistakes the nature
of those characters which are fit for far-
cical representations.

Nabobs black with crimes of the
deepest dye, are not objects to ex-
cite laughter : the magnitude of both de-
mands a more solemn audience, and points
them out as proper persons in a more seri-
ous drama. Possibly their wives, drest
out in diamonds and oriental pearls, might
not improperly blaze in the character of
the Queen of Shebah, and, with an auk-
ward display of wealth in clumsy magni-
ficence and misplaced ornaments, become
only the objects of mirth and ridicule ;
could the spectator forget that the destruction of India and infamy of Great Britain
were the price at which all this costly
finery was purchased.

Previous

' Previous to Lord Clive's vindication of the much injured and misrepresented servants of the Company in India, he gives a description of the inhabitants of Indostan, whom he represents, " especially those of Bengal, as servile, mean, submissive, and humble, in inferior stations; and in superior, luxurious, effeminate, tyrannical, treacherous, venal, cruel." Whether the contrast be so great as he would have us believe, between the servants of the Company and the Indians in superior stations, and whether those *English Gentlemen* had not adopted and improved upon the last set of Eastern qualities, will best appear in the reports of the Select and Secret Committees. But the instruction to be collected from the assertions and characters contained in the speech of the Peer and Hero of Plassey is plainly this: the enormities committed in India are all to be laid to the account of the native Indians, Guard against them by restrictions and regulations! free the servants of the Company from their tyrannic influence from which *they cannot now fly!* and all may be safely trusted to those humane *English Gentlemen,* " who were the Cabinet-Council that planned every thing, and with the Officers of the navy and army, who have had *great share* in the execution, justly claim, not only a part, but the whole merit of our great acquisitions. p. 46. It is true, indeed, that the *whole* of the inland trade, upon which depends in some degree the receipt of the revenues, and almost totally the happiness and prosperity of the people, has been taken into the hands of those meritorious servants of the Company, and of their agents, which they have carried on in a capacity before unknown; for they have traded, not only as merchants, but as sovereigns; and, by grasping at the whole of the inland trade, have taken the bread out of the mouths of thousands and thousands of merchants, who used formerly to carry on that trade, and who are now reduced to beggary. To this cause the

the diftrefs in Bengal, as far as it relates
to the inland trade, is owing." p. 48, 49.
And one inftance of that diftrefs, has been
the famine of 1770, in which many thoufands fell a facrifice to the avarice and tyranny of thofe moft *merciful* monopolifts.
But we are told, in p. 43, that " The
Company's fervants have not been the
authors of thofe acts of violence and oppreffion, of which it is the fafhion to accufe them ; and that fuch crimes are committed by the natives of the country, acting as their agents, and for the moft part
without their knowledge."

However cruel thofe agents may have
been to their unhappy countrymen, their
tendernefs and honefty towards their mafters are exemplary and unexampled, en-
riching them with the fpoil, while they
faved them from any participation of the
guilt by which it was acquired, and from
the horrors with which their *charitable,
benevolent, generous, and hofpitable fouls,*
would

would be affected by the knowledge of such abominations.

The leſſon thus taught by that noble Lord's ſpeech, is no bad ſpecimen of the advice likely to be given to your Lordſhip by any of the inferior Nabobs, ſhould any be taken into your councils, for the formation of laws properly adapted to the preſent ſtate of India.

· Adequate remedies and preventives can-not now be hoped for. A few out-lines are all that the wit of man can produce from the materials with which your Lord-ſhip is furniſhed. The reſt muſt be left, at leaſt for the preſent, to the wiſdom and integrity of thoſe who ſhall be entruſted with the adminiſtration of government in India. Speculative ſyſtems of legiſlation are hazardous; but thoſe tranſplanted from one country to another, diſſimilar in al-moſt every circumſtance, will certainly fail. A perfect plan to be formed at once, is of all imaginary entities the moſt vain and chimerical.

The

The edifice muſt riſe by flow degrees, through many alterations, ſuggeſted by trial, and approved by experience. So roſe our Gothick ſtructure, ſuperior in uſe, ſtrength, and duration, to the ſplendid productions of Greece and Rome. But ſuch a ſtructure can never be fitted to an Aſiatick climate.

A barbarous people require fewer laws, than nations excelling in the refinements of arts, taſte, and luxury. Fewer means are neceſſary to direct ignorance, than to reſtrain contrivance and invention from deviating into forbidden ways. The ideas of barbariſm, and the objects of its paſſions, are not many. But its habits, inclinations, and prejudices, are ſtronger in proportion as they are leſs diſſipated and are confined to a narrower channel. To combat theſe by compulſary laws, is a hard and ungrateful taſk. To form and mold the mind to compliance, would be more eaſy and ſucceſsful. This alone can be

effected

effected by the influence of precept, example, and kind treatment. When thefe have had their effect, laws fhould be adapted to the impreffions they have made, and to the genius and propenfities which they have created. Let the barbarian believe you love him, and mean him good; he will confide in, and be directed by you. Perfonal authority, arifing from love and reverence, muft precede laws, where tyranny is not meant to be eftablifhed; and is it poffible to fuppofe, that fuch authority can ever exift in India, in the fervants of the Company? That very title muft, for ages, render them odious; and the appellation fhould be changed, although the men were to be continued.

Ruffia is perhaps the ftrongeft inftance to be found in Hiftory, of Barbarifm humanifed, and national ignorance enlightned. By the unexampled wifdom, perfeverance, and patriotifm of one great man, followed by immediate fucceffors adopting his fyftem, fome progrefs has been made

made towards civilizing that country; and a small diſtrict ſurrounding the ſeat of the moſt extenſive European Empire, is now emerging from darkneſs. The capital has an academy, founded by the late Empreſs, where ſcience begins to dawn; and the preſent Sovereign has publiſhed an eſſay towards a code of laws. But the Ruſſians are ſtill ſlaves.

Natural as liberty is to man, ſociety ſeems ſtill more natural: all are certainly made to aſſociate; but it is not ſo clear that all are made to enjoy liberty, while two thirds of the human ſpecies, women and children, are formed ſubject to the will of others.

Where-ever the human footſtep is found, civil ſocieties are eſtabliſhed; and in every ſuch ſociety natural freedom is reſtrained either by a voluntary ſurrender, or by the exerciſe of force or cunning, qualities natural to ſome, as imbecillity, and puſillanimity, producing ſubjection, are to others:

F   In

In thofe it is natural to rife, in thefe to fink. All effects are from the operation of natural caufes, various and differing as the caufes which produce them differ and prevail. Tawny complexions are as natural in Afia, as fair are in Europe. They are not to be altered; becaufe the caufe is permanent, and whatever proceeds from that influencing principle, whether in bodily form or the affections of the mind, is equally unalterable. If the climate which tinges the Afiatick fkin unnerves the hand and heart, you may wafh the Afiaticks white as eafily as make them free.

Would to God! that the caufes which produce and preferve liberty were equally permanent and prevalent; and that other caufes equally natural, but hoftile to freedom, did not ofteneft prevail even in thofe foils and climates, where its growth feems moft natural. There are, and have been, flaves in all latitudes of the known world.

Greece

Greece and Rome were free ; Great Britain
ftill remains a third inftance, and hiftory
produces but three, of an empire compofed
of many provinces connected by laws, and
not preffed together by the grafp of arbitrary power. In Afia, there is not a fingle
trace of the fmalleft community where liberty ever prevailed. The very defire of
being free, if it ever could be fuppofed to
exift, is extinct there; and the utmoft hap-
pinefs which the multitude are capable of
receiving is from defpotifm wifely and hu-
manely exercifed. They have been fome-
times bleffed with good mafters. Let it be the
care of Great Britain, that the people under
her dominion fhall ever have fuch. Should
the authors of ruin, continued as the inftru-
ments of falvation, fhift their nature and
habitudes, the prodigy will be as great as
an empire in India, governed by the fame
laws, and enjoying the fame liberty, with
Great Britain.

F 2   I do

· I do not mean to argue that there should be no laws for direction and punishment: such are to be found in the most arbitrary governments, and none can subsist without them. The dominion exercised by the Company in India, did it deserve the name of government, would be an exception. The legislature of Great Britain will, no doubt, in time, compose a better code than could be produced by Eastern tyranny; but in the best that human wisdom can devise for Asia, more will depend upon execution than legislation: great discretionary powers must be allowed; and in the dilemma, if such existed, of being obliged to trust solely to either, good men would be preferable to the best laws. The Company have produced few such men; and by trying what they may hereafter do, an experiment which cannot succeed, you will retard, and possibly render impracticable, every future remedy.

If the writer of this letter finds that a continuance of his correspondence with
your

7

your Lordſhip may be likely to produce any benefit to the public, he will venture to lay before you and them, at leaſt, ſome general notions of what in his opinion would be preferable to the experiment which you mean to try. If it ſhould appear ſo in the eyes of the public, your Lordſhip, from a laudable deference to them, may adopt what you would not be otherwiſe induced to propoſe. This conſideration, and this alone, has determined me to publiſh what at firſt was intended for your private peruſal, by

My Lord,

Your Lordship's

Moſt humble and

Obedient Servant,

April 24th,
1773.

A. B.

www.ingramcontent.com/pod-product-compliance
Lightning Source LLC
Chambersburg PA
CBHW032141080426

42733CB00008B/1156